My Year With
Hares

Dedication

To my daughter Megan Hayward Smith for being such a good spotter of hares and geese, for enjoying my pace of life, and taking on new adventures in all elements.

And Fiona, for walking into my life across the salt marshes and sandbars, for life is a much more beautiful, calmer place with you beside me.

Freedom is space
Space is freedom

Published by Martin Hayward Smith
and produced by

Red Hare Publishing Ltd
c/o Pinkfoot Gallery, High St.,
Cley, Norfolk NR25 7RB
+44 01263 740947

info@redharepublishing.co.uk
www.redharepublishing.co.uk

ISBN: 978-0-9930293-0-1

Printed by Swallowtail Print Ltd
www.swallowtailprint.co.uk

My Year With
Hares

Martin Hayward Smith

Introduction

By Martin Hayward Smith

The first time I saw a hare was when I was just a young lad. I went out beating for the first time and as I walked across a stubble field, suddenly this large mammal got up from under my feet. We were both startled as it sprinted in the opposite direction across the landscape, something I have never forgotten.

So it is something I have always wanted to do: take time out for a year to observe and study my favourite species, the hare. I still don't quite know how I found the time, but I did.

I armed myself with my small rucksack, and within it my faithful Canon 50d, 100 to 400mm lens, and 24 to 105mm lens and kept a diary recording my experiences and adventures along the way. Somedays too, the car was my mobile hide.

At the end of the day, it would come down to one's skill of field craft and knowledge of the land, and luck. But I am very fortunate to be able to gain access to a number of private locations by local land owners in North Norfolk, with its prime UK hare habitats, from Holkham, The Barshams to Burnham Market; an area that covers many thousands of acres.

I must admit it was a wild and erratic start to the year, but as the seasons changed so did I. An inner calmness and contentment overcame me, as I followed the path of the hare and life out on the open fields, under the huge and ever-changing Norfolk sky.

Foreword

By Ray Mears

If you want to see wildlife you need to dress warmly and in colours that blend in with your surroundings. Then go outdoors when others are indoors and sit perfectly still. Remain perfectly still even if it involves suffering.

Some years ago I was sitting under an isolated oak tree in a frosty stubble barley field atop a Perthshire hill. Cloaked in the long morning shadow of the tree I was invisible, motionless, mentally defying the bone-penetrating chill. The first rays of the morning sun were doing nothing to warm my body, but they did lift my spirits as I enjoyed each broken stem of barley receiving a lick of scarlet light.

Now cold can make you sleep and just as I felt my grip on wakefulness slipping I was jolted to alertness by the passing of a buzzard right in front of me, only a metre above the ground, so close in fact that I could both hear and feel the passage of the draft from its wings. These are the moments those of us in love with nature live for, but on this particular morning the buzzard was but a herald for a more impressive player about to appear.

In front of me was a game trail passing towards me from my left front and behind me to my right rear. Just as the buzzard had passed a tiny movement drew my attention to the vanishing point of the game trail ahead of me. Slowly, so as to be invisible, I brought my 8x32's to my eyes. Now I could make out what the strange movement was, it was a pair of tall ears coming straight towards me, the ears of a Brown Hare. Almost as soon as my mind deciphered the movement, the animal's head and then body came into view hurrying towards me on his secret mission. From my vantage point I realised that where the trail vanished there was a slope, consequently the hare was emerging from the shadow of dead ground into the beautiful sunlight. As the hare crested the hill he stopped and surveyed his territory. Now in full sight I had the most glorious view of this remarkable creature. Bathed now from ear tip to toe in golden warmth, his chest puffed out and his hairs responding to a breeze so gentle that I had been unaware of it. If at that moment you had told me that this was the king of all the hares I would have believed it. As the hare looked around I was struck by the golden translucency of his eye. After a long moment he resumed his regal progress passing within touching distance of me. Amongst our native wildlife the hare is special, imbued in some strange way with a greater measure of wildness than others creatures. I love watching them and when they watch me, I sense their intelligence and the ancient heritage of their wisdom.

The following pages capture beautifully the spirit of the hare and the dedication of Martin Hayward Smith, a remarkable naturalist and wildlife cameraman – who you can be certain has sat still and suffered for his art. It is a privilege to write this foreword and rather fitting as in many ways it was a hare that first provided me with the opportunity to work alongside Martin.

Particularly in the early spring, hares can be called up by mimicking the squeak of an injured leveret. Employing this trick while filming for the first series of ITV's Wild Britain, I called to a Suffolk hare four hundred metres away. Responding to instinct the hare raced straight to me stopping only five metres away. Sadly the cameraman of the day failed to capture the event. Not because of any lack of skill but because he was not a naturalist and did not realise what was about to happen. Consequently in the next season I was fortunate to be teamed with two wildlife cameramen including Martin. If I am honest I was a little dubious, so frequently TV exaggerates claims of expertise. But from the moment I first watched Martin take quietly to the shadows of a hedgerow with his camera I realised the depth of his experience and great fieldcraft. Moreover he has that special something; nature responds to him, so evident one morning on the Isle of Wight when a Stoat dashed up to him bearing the gift of a dead Rabbit, all of course captured on camera.

This book is Martin's tribute to the Brown Hare, but more it stands as testimony to both his skill and his hopeless love for nature. But then why not, for none of the world's riches can compare with the wealth that comes from allowing nature so deeply into your life.

Spring

12th February

I have been very fortunate with my job as a wildlife cameraman as it has taken me to many beautiful parts of the planet. But for the next six weeks I have a commission to make a film on hares. How lucky is that, making a programme about my favourite mammal. I will have a four person production crew with me, which could prove challenging as I find it hard enough with just me sneaking about, trying not to disturb my subject. It will be one and a half months straight through. No days off, just live, sleep and breathe hares. Let's go make a film.

13th February

Sitting in my bespoke hide in a hedgerow gap I can sit with the partridges dust bathing along the hedge to my right with the hares just out in front of me. I say 'bespoke', as most commercially available hides are three feet square. I still use one from time to time, but being six foot two, after 12 hours in a hide I have to make sure there is no-one around, un-zip the back and roll out like a diver off the side of a boat. Once laying there I have to uncoil myself, hence my hides are now made slightly bigger, so that I can stretch out with enough room for my filming equipment. I love being in a hide, disappearing into the landscape.

14th February

A good start to the filming project, and so special to be on my own patch, but I still have to deliver. It's great to be able to show hares in a landscape, a picture within a picture. They are boxing, but it's all a bit too distant at the moment to film slow motion 'wow' shots; nonetheless it's still great to witness. I know in my gut that I will soon have them fighting in front of my lens. It will happen.

16th February

For the past three days I have been sitting in a hide and seeing nothing. I have a migraine powering in, so today I will go out hunting when all I really want to do is climb into a dark hole, but time will not allow. It's not always out there on a plate like in a zoo and it does not always go to plan. I do not think the hares have read the script, know to perform in front of the hide and to run in from the right, box, then exit on the left! As mid-day passes and still nothing, I realise I must drink some water. It is mid afternoon and the sun will soon be disappearing over the horizon. I take one last look down the cart track in the opposite direction. The sun is on my back. I stop and listen. I can hear a male Grey Partridge calling out in the last of the sun's rays, and there it is, caught on film. Well worth four days of nothing, to paint this glorious bird in such wonderful light.

17th February

Some of the fields are so vast you can see why the hares feel safe in them, and some days they are so far away that observing and filming are just impossible. It's a case of sit tight and wait until they come to you. On the next field over the hedge is the same crop of sugar beet which has just been lifted, and I can hear thousands of Pink-footed Geese dropping in. That will be my next port of call.

18th February

Last night the weather forecast said that there would be a sharp frost but promised a sunny start to the day. I drove down beside the triangle field hoping to see the hares out chasing on one of my favourite patches. I soon realised that I would lose the golden light, what we film-makers call the golden hour. I headed the car back through the gate and onto the track, where I was met by two male Grey Partridges fighting. They were oblivious to my presence as they carried on their tirade with beaks and claws. A third bird then came rushing in but then thought better of it and carried on by. The stronger of the males would not give up on his female or territory, so after one final chase the intruder took flight.

25th February

Up and out; it's misty but the sun should burn it off later. I have a rough idea where to go to get dew-ladened cobwebs strewn across the field. It's like pea-soup out here as I drive down the tracks and out onto the stubble field. I ease the vehicle into position so that I will face directly into the sun.

Luckily it all went to plan. As the sun heated up the stubble you could hear it snap, crackle and pop. Time for a cup of char.

26th February

As I sit in the field today, I can't help think how quintessentially English it is to look over a beautiful landscape with Grey Partridges calling to each other in the background. It is such a beautiful bird, one I have grown to love and respect. I was introduced to these birds by Herbert Palmer, an old gamekeeper on the Houghton Estate. He was a real gentleman and would take me out nesting along the vast hedgerows, snapping a twig here and there to mark where the female partridges were sitting on their nests; a dedicated guardian of these birds.

27th February

As I look deep into the golden-agate eyes of a Brown Hare, I try to understand the mystical beliefs associated with it and why many of us find it so alluring with its shape, form and tales. I'm thinking that after the filming commission on hares, I will stay on the land for the next year to follow the hare though the changing seasons, and see where it takes me.

3rd March

Sometimes while out with my camera looking for leverets (young hares) in the stubble fields, I use my flask to mark the tramlines where I have spotted one in the distance. I carry on hunting for others. These lines are then marked with sticks as I place my hide in a nearby hedge, to wait and observe. While in my hide I have seen many tractor drivers stop to place the young leverets onto the newly turned-over soil as they plough up the land.

I often wonder, when I find a single leveret, how it got there. The mother would have given birth to her offspring in the nest, so I wonder would she pick them up individually in her mouth and place them away from the nest on their own, or do the young scuttle out of their own accord, away from where they were born? It makes perfect sense that they are not all in one nest, as that would make it just too easy for predators.

4th March

Mrs S from a nearby Estate called in yesterday evening to look at the hare pictures and some of the writing. Much was discussed as to the lay of the land. Recently, when out horse riding, she had noticed several dead hares. When I managed to catch up with Richard, the gamekeeper, later that day, he had seen the same thing. Hares are prone to certain diseases including dysautonomia, coccidiosis and yersinosis.

5th March

Out on the long fields, I watch a male hare going up to a female to check to see if she is in, or coming into, season. This is when it could all kick off with fur flying, turning into a boxing match. Instead he leaves her in peace and carries on travelling his home boundaries, stopping now and again to sniff and check for any female odours on the stems of the stubble. It's one of those things you observe when you are out in the field. Another male on the same quest joins him as they both hop up through the hedge on the scent of a female.

8th March

Time to head back in as I am now getting more picky about what I film. I love to paint with light, so when I turned the corner and saw these three hares feeding on the side of the hill and casting long shadows, I pulled the car in off the dirt track behind a hedge. I slowly got the equipment out and managed to film through a gap, with them blissfully unaware of me. So it's now to Wells-next-the-Sea for fish and chips on the quay, and some fresh salty air.

9th March

I have been sitting here with this pair of hares for three hours now. The male is known as the buck and the female as the doe or jill. He will be her guardian and has been with her now for seven days in this particular location. With the doe in season he is waiting for the time when she is fertile to be mated with, which only happens on a few occasions each year. Today is one of those days. I am lucky as, so far, there are no other males in the vicinity. I don't want them to get chased down over the brow of the hill and out of sight. While I have been watching this pair, they have mated nine times but not always successfully. With his over-eagerness, there were many times she lowered her head, raised her haunches and launched him skywards. With that, she would move away for several metres and lie down, the buck likewise. It's so easy to lose them in the landscape; I only have to turn away for a few seconds to look out for other hares approaching, otherwise I will need to search for my courting couple all over again.

10th March

In Norfolk there are still good numbers of hares to be seen. They are on the well-drained high ground or the crop patchwork and wide field margins that are in stewardship schemes. It is known that hares do not do so well in big blocks of monoculture or in the West Country, where pasture land with cattle predominates. I also know that gamekeepers play their part, for in the thousands of acres I am allowed to go over, there are hardly any foxes. It has got to be good news for the young leverets over the spring, as they do not get mopped up of a night time and are given the chance to survive.

11th March

On the go now for ten hours. I pull in off the road and enter a field. I slowly cross over the stubble field and see the quarry backlit with the sun, which will be setting soon. I angle the car and switch off the engine. I know the score; do not move, just hide behind the camera and wait. Pheasants cross the field, a pair of Grey Partridges feed along the old tramline next to the car, and even the Skylarks are calling it a day. But I feel as if mine has just begun so I sit still. The odd hare hops by, and some stop to feed and wash. Others just go by, no rush. Not wanting to move my lens, I stay fixed with the hare next to me laying in a form. At some point, it will have to get up and stretch. It has breathing space. I just have to wait a little longer.

12th March

Oystercatchers are piping away on an oilseed rape field. I watch an amazing battle between a male and female hare, which lasted for ages. Eventually they mate and then lie down in the stubble field some two metres apart, as other young bucks run up and down the field with their noses to the ground trying to pick up her scent. The pair lay flat but one young buck picked up her scent and headed in, to be chased off by the dominant male. Close by is another female with two males in pursuit; now five of them are running across field after field. Two more males are criss-crossing the field with noses to the ground. I am sitting in my car on top of a hill, looking down into a bowl, which is just like an arena. Another pair run in and mate; that's three couples in an hour. The sun is shining but there is a cold gusting wind cutting across the hilltops and I have twelve hares around me. Now with two fights going on, it's time to start my vehicle and get closer. What a fight, fur going everywhere.

13th March

It always amuses me that when hares are chasing and males are in hot pursuit of a female in season, she can go to ground and give them the slip. It's then that you get the males, like these five, going back to the area she was last seen and sniffing the ground to try and pick up her scent.

14th March

All is quiet for the male and female hare on guard back to back, with the doe on the left more relaxed. The silence is broken with the sudden shrill of a cock Pheasant's piercing call as a jet fighter flies though the sound barrier.

15th March

It is now quarter past nine and I have been on the hunt for the past three hours. Today is grey and overcast with not a single hare in sight. I turn into the wheat field, off the cart track and there in front of me are five hares boxing. I swing the car round, switch on the new filming camera that arrived yesterday evening, but nothing happens. I move the car, turn off the engine and grapple with the camera, which is still giving me trouble. Why is life like this? I take the camera from its tripod, switch over dials, replace it, and you've guessed it, the hares have gone. Today is going downhill rapidly!

16th March

I think it's Thursday. I've now been on this shoot for twenty days, thirteen hours per day. It's all becoming a blur. It has been foggy now for the past four days, a bit like my head. The late afternoon light is very flat, I have developed a migraine and there are too many questions from the production crew. I just wonder what ever happened to field craft and ethics. It's now almost five in the afternoon and a hazy sun is trying to burn through for the first time in days. There are now three hares coming out of a small copse; time to go to work.

17th March

I had to smile to myself today while stalking a hare. The feel wasn't quite right, so I put my binoculars up to my eyes. It was a large flint. Glad nobody was with me!

18th March

Sitting on top of high hill in the fog and I can hardly see a damn thing. Nearby a pair of male Pheasants are going at each other hammer and tongs. Four hares suddenly break through the hedge and run across the newly set wheat. I sit gazing out onto a blank canvas. In front there is no form or composition, just emptiness, a void in time. I must press on before the darkness closes in.

19th March

It feels like the first day of spring. As I look through my office window onto the garden, the Robin is singing at full throttle. The Daffodils stand proud as there is no wind and the sun has warmed enough to wake the odd Peacock butterfly. I have been looking at a computer screen for five hours, going through several thousand pictures for what could be a new project. Sarah called to check that I was still sitting at my desk sorting images but fifteen minutes later I was in my car with my camera beside me. Well, it was lunchtime so I went for a drive up to the high field to look out across Norfolk.

For once there are no hares to be seen. I got near to the top of the hill and passed one hare in a form, soaking up the sun. I turned the car around at the top and headed back down. Halfway down the track I decided to go back to sit with the hare. I stayed with him for forty minutes, filling the frame. It was then that I noticed two hares giving chase as they came over the top of the hill from my left. They started boxing and I was locked in. He was very keen but she was having none of it, and they ran to my right, keeping close, now with a copse behind them. He tried to get closer to sniff, and at this point they stood up on their hind legs and she knocked seven bells out of him, fur flying everywhere. She spun sideways after what seemed like a lifetime of boxing and was out of there. They ran to my left and out of sight through the hedge. I sat there elated for what I had just captured on camera; it was spell-binding.

You can see why they call them Mad March hares with their boxing and frolics, especially this time of year when the vegetation is so sparse, making it easy to observe their courting rituals.

I winked at the hare still in the form near the car and thanked her for being there. I drove back home punching the air, right place, right time and some luck.

20th March

Driving across the North Norfolk countryside looking for hares, I feel like a hare myself, jinking across the vast landscape. I pull in somewhere to make phone calls and all is well with the world. I'm now off to West Norfolk, to meet a farmer who's going to take me out to see his land. I now have another patch, some 1500 acres, with hares everywhere. Mark's parents have leverets in their walled garden every year and it is fantastic to gaze at a field and see twenty hares.

21st March

I phoned Richard to ask if he had found any leverets. He said he had but they'd been predated, but was I still interested in the blue hare, as it had re-appeared on a stubble field? He gave me the co-ordinates, but it was raining so I decided to wait until tomorrow; I didn't want to get bogged down in the vehicle.

Next day I pulled through the gate into a new field that I hadn't previously visited as it had busy roads running either side of it. Looking through my binoculars I could see that the remaining two sides were fenced with rabbit netting; a small, confined field compared to what I have been used to driving over. I could see where Richard had driven so decided to follow his tracks. Grey Partridges continued to hunt for food and I could see the odd hare anchored down in their forms as I drove slowly past. Suddenly, there it was, running along the top of the field. My first blue hare! There are many different colour variations that you can find from time to time, a throw back in the genes. Now and again you get this result, which is nothing to do with the Mountain Hare. You only have to look at the ears on a Brown Hare, which are much longer and do not have the rounded tips of their northern cousins.

I photographed two shots of it in the distance as a record and then turned the car around. The hare was very skittish and it ducked into the hedge with the road on the other side, cars roaring past. I sat with my heart in my mouth; this was going to be harder than I thought. I pulled back and watched it run back up to the top of the field, through a tiny gap into the next field and away. At this point so was I. I would try again over many more days but sadly to no avail. It had vanished.

Later I drove back onto the same field. I glimpsed something to my right and there it was, only two metres away, hunched down in its form. I would have to circle round and come in from a wider angle if it were to tolerate my presence. Ideally I would have liked to put a hide up on the field but it was too open to the roads and would have drawn too much attention. I crept the car forward, scraping over the stubble, making too much noise. I managed to pull alongside but kept the engine running. I was able to take four shots before driving away to leave him or her in peace, in the hope that Blue would not be startled towards the road.

I was smitten with what I had seen.

22nd March

I am sitting writing this in a hole in a hawthorn hedge, lying in the shade, looking out over a field of wheat. The sun is shining and it is wall to wall blue sky. My second Brimstone has just flown by; I saw my first on Saturday 19th March. The Blackthorn is now in flower and finally it feels like spring, with the earth warming up.

I am so lucky to be observing this, with a flask of Earl Grey to hand and the sun on my back. Pheasants are calling out and a Yellowhammer is singing. At times like this you wish there was someone else to share all of this with. Now a pair of buzzards glide into view, circling above with their piercing cries.

I notice nine hares in front of me, with one female obviously in season. The dominant male now is having a really hard time boxing off the other bucks. Suddenly it turns wild as nine hares chase and circle the field. They run to my right towards the hedge and then with a sudden twist, run along the hedge towards me. I freeze as the Grand National hurtles past. One of them slips through the hedge next to me, I lift my camera and photograph the last one as it goes by. She then leads them all the way down the hedge and loses some of them in the next field. I remember the sounds of their feet charging by on the dry soil, dust being kicked up. Several males return to the field running with their noses to the ground, sniffing for her scent and searching. My heart is pounding, and I had to call someone. I phone Sarah, a good friend, and exploded down the phone. She was slightly quieter at her end for she was standing over Adders!

23rd March

I have just watched a Sparrowhawk glide through a hedge like silk; to me they are the Spitfires of the sky, buzzards are like Lancaster bombers and harriers are the Focke-Wulfs. I am amazed by how many Curlews are out on these inland fields, along with Shelducks, Golden Plovers and Oystercatchers. Should they not be up at the coast? I can honestly say that today I am lost in a silent world. God, do I need to get out! Next Friday, 10 days from now, this commission will end. I need to 'blow out' big time, to run wild like the hare.

24th March

Blue skies and another warm day with no wind, this is just brilliant. Today I have a team up from Devon to fly the Skybot, a small remote-controlled drone with a high definition camera on the front. I want a completely different angle on things for this production. The drone is able to fly at 65 miles an hour and reach heights of 400 feet. We set off in convoy, passing fields with a few hares in, but I wanted a female in season with the dominant male, plus a few other bucks waiting in the wings. After several miles of hunting, I had found what I needed and we pulled up alongside the hedge, peering through the branches. The female was lying there eating with the dominant male keeping the other two males at bay. We would only have one chance at this as it was a lucky find. Chris, who was responsible for flying the Skybot fired it up and Jonathan was in position to operate the controls of the camera. As the drone went up high, the other males got brave and went in for the female, so the chase was on. Then Skybot came down lower and hovered over the action. Much to everybody's surprise, it worked!

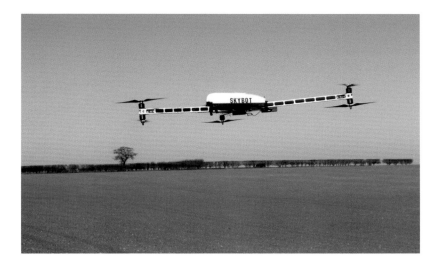

25th March

In bed and my head is wired, buzzing with ideas for this hare program. I am always thinking of scripts, sequences, form and composition and what would be good right now is hares in front of a church. Great to push things to the edge, so I set myself a challenge. It took some time to travel around Norfolk with my ordnance survey maps but I found the perfect spot and for several days I filmed hares chasing one another in front of the church tower. Bliss.

26th March

Once again I am sitting on top of the high hill in the rain but at least I have some peace and quiet. Grey skies all around and the rain is set in for some time, backed up by a driving wind. The farmers will be happy as there has been no rain for the past 29 days. This hill has become my sanctuary; a place to clear my head. And then in the distance, a jogger with a bright red top! No peace for the wicked. I am on the phone but I wave, she smiles back and then heads off back down the hill. When she is passing for the third time I open my window and we introduce ourselves. I then watch Cathy run back down the hill again in the rain; everyone needs their own space. In the distance a pair of hares can be seen mating in the next field. A glimmer of sunshine on the horizon means it is time to go in close.

27th March

Some 40 Fieldfares are moving along the stubble field; soon they will be flying back across the water to Scandinavia. Heading along the cart track I check out the forms. I have come to know where the individual hares are laying and pulling up alongside one of them, I look down the lens and I notice this one is bloodied. It is near to the road so I cannot help but think it has been hit by a car. The following morning, the form lays empty.

29th March

Today I measured out an area of 63 by 30 metres to mark out the hare forms. Hares do not burrow but make a small depression or scrape in the ground, the back of which is wider and deeper than the front. This is where they will sleep and rest in rain, hail, snow and heat. This hollow is known as a form, and they lay as flat as possible with their ears held horizontal along their back, blending into the surroundings. Within this area I marked out 38 forms with red flags, some old and some new.

In this fresh form you can see the claw marks where the hare pushed itself out at speed; think of starting blocks for the hundred metres. Also in the form you can see some droppings; hares are known to have eaten their own pellets. Also it's the time of year when you will find many dead hares along the roadside, where they have chased after one another across the fields, onto the tarmac and into traffic.

31st March

The wind has picked up one of my bespoke two man hides, and has rolled it into the next-door neighbour's field of oilseed rape. The damn thing was so well pegged down, all I can do is take the canvas off and put the frame back into place. It really is getting worse as I drive back down the road. I am hit by a sandstorm. It's like being back in the Wahiba sands, the light soil on the land is just blowing across the land and not a hare in sight. I know just where they will be. I am sure there will be some of them in the woods with their backs up against the trees. Would you lay out there in that wind when you could be in the shelter of the woods?

1st April

Crunch time, as I now need to find some leverets, but where to start? I phoned around, speaking to eight keepers, putting a hefty reward down for finding some. Ten days pass and nothing, so it is now time for me to join the hunt. It's not easy and more days drift by. I find the odd singleton, most of which are about two weeks old.

As time for the production is coming to an end, the pressure is on.

Then, late one afternoon I rejoice when I find a nest of four young leverets just a few days old. A female can give birth to three or four litters per year, each of two to four young, occasionally five. They are born fully furred with their eyes open. These youngsters will be weaned by about four weeks old. The infra-red filming that night, with the female coming into let the young suckle, was amazing.

2nd April

It's my birthday and for a change I will go and sit with the hares! I pass sleeping hares and partridges dozing in the warmth of the spring sunshine. I settle down with three hares. From what I can make out there is a female asleep at the back and the nearest one is another female feeding being watched over by a male. A Long-tailed Tit keeps flying into the hedge in the same place; I will have to check that out later. The male hare tries it on with the female and the chase is on. They stay just in front of me, as I have disappeared from their world. She claws at him and fur floats off in the light breeze. He tries again but to no avail as she is not ready. What amuses me is that the female at the back takes hardly any notice, even when the other two fight in her space.

3rd April

Where has the past month and a half gone? I have been spending so much solid time with these remarkable creatures. I have learnt, studied and witnessed so many breath-taking moments. It has been 24/7 with the hares.

The footage has been amazing and I am now looking forward to the final edit; just a shame it is not for British television. I have placed a script about hares with the BBC Natural History Unit, so maybe one day.

But now I have to take down my tower and the hides on the stubble fields, for they are about to be ploughed in readiness for potatoes. Then I must go and say thank you to all those who were involved. And then off for a recce for a new programme with Jimmy Docherty and up to the Cairngorms to do some filming with Ray Mears. And guess what? We are looking for Mountain Hares! That should be wicked!

4th April

Last night on the forecast it stated that there would be gale force winds, and they were not wrong! As I drive down the dry dirt tracks there is dust everywhere and as I turn the corner it is like being in a sand storm. The top soil is so dry that it is just being picked up and carried on the wind. A Red Kite goes screaming by but not a hare in sight. I creep into Half Moon Wood and sure enough there is a hare with its back up against a tree, facing down wind, sheltering from the storm. Nothing stirs, every creature hunkered down.

19th April

As I watch a lone hare run at speed across the Norfolk landscape, I cannot help but think of a story told of Queen Boudicca, ruler of the Iceni people of East Anglia. Before the battle with the Romans, she released a hare from under her gown, and in which direction it ran, that would be the path that she led her army into battle. It would make a good sketch for Monty Python.

20th April

I knew I had too much to drink at a dinner party last night, but it was good to be with friends, laugh and be entertained. I have been so immersed with hares of late, maybe I will see people again in a month's time. Today I will just go and sit on the edge of a field with a bottle of water to drink. I have quite a few hares feeding around me, and I watch with amusement as a Stoat runs across the field. It gets close to a feeding hare, who does not stop to look up but carries on eating. It would have been a different story had it been a Rabbit.

21st April

I condense the shot through my faithful 100-400mm lens, and squeeze the bright colours of the tulip blooms into the frame, like looking down a kaleidoscope with psychedelic, vibrant patterns. It's half six in the morning and the sun is just coming up over the tree lines. I am sitting with Chris Knights, as we look down across a field with the odd hare, trying to avoid the large irrigation system used to water the flowers, no doubt soaking the newborn leverets hiding amongst the stems.

I have heard many tales from my elders about a man called Kenzie, a colourful character who lived out in the Fens. He could 'call up' hares, especially those females who have newborns nearby. Chris had learnt this call from Kenzie; it was like a distress call but not at all like squeaking a Stoat up. I sat there in his vehicle transfixed. Although I had witnessed this lots of times before in our 30 year friendship, it still amazed me how a hare could sprint up to Chris and run underneath the vehicle. I went back to the field that evening with my daughter to show her the spectacle of colour and started to teach her how to 'call up' the hare, passing the art on to the next generation. As the light faded, we headed back to base but could not resist the last shot of hares out in a wheat field and the Roe Deer passing by them at dusk.

22nd April

Checked along the potato fields and saw nothing. Suddenly a pair of male pheasants burst into the air from out of one of the deep furrows, fighting; it's like something from out of The Matrix. These birds have spurs on the back of their legs to hack at each other with vicious downward blows. It's all about territorial disputes, which are more intense during the breeding season. Tell me about it!

23rd April

Mr & Mrs S. came round last night to look at the images that I had photographed. It was good to share what I had seen on their land. Mr S. commented on the number of hares in one shot and told me that a group is known as a Huske. You learn something new every day!

24th April

I often wonder how hares have coped with man as we have changed their environment. We have put roads across fields where they once ran freely and deep furrows across potato fields, which I suppose make good wind breaks but are not good to chase over. They have had to adapt to vast acres of crops covered in plastic sheeting and they will have to contend with more as our population expands with ever more mouths to feed.

25th April

It's Easter, and a buck stands guard over his doe, casting his eye over the land in case another suitor comes running in and has to be boxed away. As you can see, in most of the shots of the couples, the female is the larger of the two.

Originally it was the Easter Hare and not the Easter Rabbit, the hare being a symbol of fertility connected with the Anglo-Saxon goddess Eostre and her pagan rites of fertility and the coming of spring.

29th April

Had company with me today while searching for hares; artist Rachael Lockwood came along to take photographs for references. We managed to find some on the last remaining stubble field, and two hares boxing in the distance were a real treat to watch. As we were driving off the field the car jerked, the back shock absorber gave in and it felt like we were at sea, rocking up and down. We had spent an hour and half looking for hares but it was time to let the field settle down.

We drove off the high top fields in sunshine with clear blue skies. Skylarks were singing high above, hares lying in forms next to the track and Oystercatchers were piping out in the spring wheat. Soon the hares would be lost in the crops and out of sight for months to come. With not much happening we headed back down the hill and cut right alongside a field and then between two gate posts and up along a newly ploughed field. Suddenly six hares came running our way. Off goes the engine, camera at the ready. Four of the hares ran back over the ridge, while the front pair kept coming, the male intent on the female. Within the next second they were mating at which point my camera stopped. The card was full! I struggled to get the flash card out and find another. All I could hear was Rachel taking pictures; I could not even glance up, as I did not want to see what I was missing. It was not until Rachel stopped, that I looked up and saw two hares run to the back of the car and disappear though the hedge. Someone behind me was very happy indeed, although upset for me, but that's life. I was too engrossed to notice the card getting full. I looked forward to seeing her paintings after spending four hours with the hares. We celebrated with ginger beer and ginger biscuits.

Summer

1st May

I opened my door to a sunny day and refilled the puddle outside my cottage with more top soil. As I drove out the Swallows and House Martins swooped straight in for the mud. My quest today was a simple one, although looking back I was lucky. I wanted a hare in the English landscape, with the yellow of an oilseed rape field somewhere in the background. I sat downwind of a hare all day in a warm, gentle breeze so it couldn't catch my scent. Just as well I had some of my daughter Megan's renowned flapjacks with me. I just wanted to show a hare again amid the rich tapestry of colour made by the different crops, for which they are so well suited. There are still no sightings or word of the elusive blue hare, and there will be no chance to spot it with the crops growing and the vegetation around the hedges and field margins getting ever higher. I wonder if the blue hare is still alive and if it mated and passed on its genes.

2nd May

The swathe of plastic over the crops is vast and when the wind blows, it gives it a rippling effect, like a large lake. I watch a pair of courting hares chasing each other over yet another man made obstacle.

3rd May

I am sitting in my hide by a Lapwing's nest in a meadow, next to the River Stiffkey, which is also a good area for hares. Suddenly the Lapwing flies away; is it something I have done? There's an awful lot of calling by the bird as a Carrion Crow walks in, cocks its head, glares at my lens, and then proceeds up to the nest. Instead of flying away with the eggs, which I have previously witnessed, it eats them there and then.

4th May

Over at Chris's today for a drive around Breckland, with its pine trees and light, sandy soil. It is amazing that just a few miles down the road the habitat can change dramatically, but this is also a good place for hares. It is not long before we came upon a recently sprayed field and it is always a shame when you see the birds like Skylarks and Lapwings that depend on the insects and grubs to feed their young. We found a Lapwing's nest with hares feeding close by. I am sure that if there were pheasants nearby, the Lapwing would have been off its nest, dive bombing, calling out and trying to move them on as fast as possible. We then went onto another field to move a hide closer to a Stone Curlew nest. It will take five moves to get the hide into its correct position and for the birds to get used to it. For the next two days I am filming here with Ray Mears.

As I was leaving the parched Brecks, with dust everywhere and irrigation pipes running from one end of the field to the other, it was hard not to notice the approaching storm in the distance. The rain should keep the farmers happy.

7th May

The hares are still running and chasing and I am sitting in the hedge, with a Cuckoo calling in the background. Two hares run right up to me and the male spots me and sits down. The female continues towards me, gets close, sees me, and then bolts to the right. I cannot get it right all of the time but I try. Maybe I should have been further back in the hedge.

8th May

Another hot day and I really ought to cut the grass at some point, but I have got to get out there looking for hares. I suppose I do not have to, but it is hard to explain; it's like a fix, just sitting and observing these creatures gets them under your skin. You never tire of the searching, watching and wonderment at these amazing, elusive animals. I have now been doing this for some 25 years, yet there is still so much more that I want to see and learn. I know there are some things I won't see, might never see in my lifetime but, as they say, that's life.

12th May

Some mornings there isn't a plan. Just get up at dawn, make a flask of tea and head out. I drive off down the cart tracks onto a high ridge to survey the land stretched out in front and listen. I lift up my binoculars to scan the fields and horizons again and again and so the waiting game begins. Then in the distance I notice a low-flying speck; it's a Marsh Harrier hunting for its quarry. An adult hare stands its ground as the harrier flies straight towards it, but the harrier is in search of leverets. I have heard many stories of adult hares trying to jump up and box a harrier as it struggles to take flight with a leveret between its talons.

13th May

There is a story about a couple of keepers in the Brecks, who were leaning on the bonnet of a Landrover and chatting. In the distance they saw two male Red-legged Partridges having a scrap, when along came a hare and started boxing them! The partridges went off on their separate ways and the hare hopped off too. The keepers were bemused by this and went over to inspect where it all took place. There in the grass lay a leveret; the hare was only trying to protect its young.

21st May

The sun has just come up and I am watching the Barn Owl hunting over the water meadow that Richard is restoring to its former glory; digging out the drains and taking out the poplar trees. It is also a good haunt for hares, but as I cock my head to one side to listen, I hear a sound that I have not heard for some time. High above me a Snipe is drumming.

It's the noise made as the bird plunges at 45 degrees, with its tail fanned out so that the two outer feathers vibrate in the wind. I stand mesmerized, gazing upward at the sky and grinning as cars pass by. I can feel their glares; maybe I have lost the plot but it is truly a magnificent sight. Believe me!

23rd May

Caught up with one of the old boys today out on the land. He asked what I was doing and I told him I was filming Brown Hares. 'Oh', he said, 'you mean the Stubble Stag'. He then started to reel off all the other local names by which the hare is known. So with pen and paper from my rucksack I wrote them down; The Stubble Stag, The Long Lugs, The Stook Deer, Frisky Legs, The Wild One, The Skipper, The Hug-the-Ground and The Lurke.

25th May

It was an early start before dawn, driving up to the hide tucked in a hedge in a corner of the field. I unloaded all the equipment outside the hide, drove half a mile back down the track, parked up and walked back to my office. There I re-arranged things inside, sat down, eased the camera lens through the porthole and sat back in my chair, listening to the male Yellowhammers singing. I was sitting opposite a hedge, a hare run disappearing into it and out onto the lane the other side.

Once again, I was playing the waiting game. Later that afternoon I was alerted by bird alarm calls and there to my left, coming down the hedge as bold as brass, was a fox carrying a Grey Partridge. I composed my shot but only took about six frames for I knew that I had the image I wanted. I love hide work, for you never know what you are going to see. It is not until afterwards that I wondered if that partridge was sitting on a clutch of eggs in the hedgerow.

6th June

The rich tapestry of the North Norfolk landscape heading up to the coast is the ideal habitat for the hare, with its acres of arable farmland. From ground level in early summer, the vast yellow sea of oilseed rape can look too intense, but from the air a patchwork of different crops is revealed.

10th June

I got a call from my friend Chris in the Brecks. The night before he had photographed leverets suckling, and he asked if I would like to join him tonight? I have been lucky enough to catch this rare spectacle on film, but never to photograph it. Female hares only suckle their young once a day, normally when the sun has just gone down and the event only lasts for a few minutes. The female will approach slowly towards the field margin where the youngsters have been laying up, and only when she feels safe will she go in. She can feed up to five leverets on her eight teats over a period of about five weeks.

That evening we set up our hides down the dusty track before six, and I even got to borrow Chris' 500mm lens. Hares and partridges came and went and Stoats ran across the track. I was happy to be in my one-metre square world and the birds began to quieten down for the end of the day. It was about three hours later, around nine, that a young leveret appeared on the track in front of us. It hopped to and fro, nibbled the grass on the verge, but was in a frivolous mood. It shot off to the other side, and a Grey Partridge, which must have been nesting nearby, appeared from nowhere, chasing the youngster into the long grass. A few seconds later both emerged to sit next to each other on the short grass, the interloper having been put in its place. The partridge then wandered off with its head held high. I was just about to sit back in my seat, when an adult hare appeared on the path, which was obviously mum as the leveret went into suckle. She was having none of it and boxed the little fellow off. It was not his lucky evening as the mother headed down the winding track with leveret in hot pursuit, watched not only by us but also by the doe Roe Deer standing close by.

13th June

It's not hard to note the changes of some adult hares between May and September. Many of them are moulting and taking on varied patterns and markings on their muzzles.

18th June

Early summer is a season of mixed blessings for wildlife, but for every tragedy there's also a sigh of relief. I'm lucky enough to be able to film and photograph at Sculthorpe Moor nature reserve, the flagship of the Hawk and Owl Trust and a wonderful place to watch nature. I helped to put a camera on the nest of a Marsh Harrier this year and watched as the female brought a mixture of food to the young. Today we had a shock when we watched as a leveret was dropped down for the three hungry chicks to pull apart. I just hope it wasn't the one I spent so much time with yesterday.

19th June

I have been commissioned to film Grey Partridges hatching. Most nests are tucked away at the bottom of a hedge surrounded by nettles, never to be seen, but now and again the odd female nests out in the open. When Chris said he found such a nest, we made a plan to erect a hide. The gamekeeper parked his Landrover across the field margin, with him nearest the nest. This allowed me to get out the other side undetected as I assembled the hide. This was to be repeated many times. By habit, I would get into the hide at dawn and be collected at dusk. I would sit there for nine hours and at three o'clock every afternoon the partridge would make a slight movement. This was my cue to start filming as she got up from her clutch, stretched her legs and wings and flew over the hedge to feed. Likewise I would quickly move things around in my hide and re-arrange camera angles and wait for her to return and settle down again on her 13 eggs. I was informed they were due to hatch out during Royal Ascot week. The male joined the female for the first time on hatching day, after approximately 24 days incubation, as it is also his duty to help look after the chicks. It always amazes me that the male knows the due date and as they hatch the female stacks all the empty shells into one and other. By mid-day they had all hatched, left the nest site and were feeding alongside the game cover. Later they moved into the tall grass and were gone.

20st June

It has been raining hard all night and day and I would love to be out there on the fields but I know I will get stuck. Even the Swallows on the line outside my bathroom window look fed up with the situation.

21st June

I watched a pair of Grey Partridges with chicks feeding on an open, short-grassed field. They were in a dangerous situation as they went about their business. All of a sudden they huddled tightly together and one of them glanced skywards. At that, so did I, and high up above was a Red Kite circling. I watched for a time before the family took sanctuary in the hedge.

22nd June

There are many times that I will watch a hare stand bolt upright on its hind legs just to get a better look across a field or down a track. High above Swallows and Swifts slice though the air.

23rd June

Today I am with Nigel again from the Hawk and Owl Trust, checking out more Marsh Harrier nests. I have a license from Natural England to film these birds at the nest, one of only two granted each year. I am amazed at the number of dead leverets being brought into the three different nest sites.

24th June

Hares prefer open arable land and well drained soil; the large acres of wheat and barley where they can sit in their forms in the middle of the field, and see danger approaching from any angle.

Along with other wildlife they have benefitted from the new field margins, part of the Countryside Stewardship Scheme. These provide much cover and a safe haven for the newborn leverets, away from the preying eyes of raptors and the lurking Fox. One of the estates that I frequent has large swathes of mixed wild flowers bordering the headlands, which are a lifeline for insects.

14th July

Had to make and film a scarecrow for a BBC production. I was able to place it in the field to the front of my cottage, so I could keep an eye on him from my bathroom window. The birds ignored this bold figure and just kept glancing upwards before continuing to feed.

18th July

Summer holidays for Megan. Today we will hunt down the old cart tracks and then take a picnic up to the house boat, leaving cameras behind.

I have wanted this shot for ages. I see this time and again, pull up and either one will hop off, or the space between them is too great. So to have hare and rabbit together, to really appreciate the differences is fantastic. With that done it is now off to the boat. Might just grab a bottle of wine on the way.

29th July

A warm summer's evening with a heady fragrance in the air, as I sat out in one of Norfolk Lavender's fields in full bloom. The sun was setting in front of me, and thousands of insects danced over the back lit purple haze of flower heads.

I have been here over many years, so it comes as no surprise to me to see families of Grey Partridges with young taking up residence, exploiting the richly abundant insect life. But also living in harmony amongst the scented rows of plants are hares that have taken sanctuary alongside the many buzzing, pollinating bees.

30th July

Another scorching hot day. I have not looked at the weather forecast for days as it is becoming predictable, like filming under big, blue African skies. As I go out, I put more water in a puddle at the front of the house so that the Swallows and House Martins can carry on collecting mud. Before I know it, about 40 birds come down. I drive down one of the cart tracks with dust trailing behind me, windows shut so as not to let it in and onto my camera. There are potato fields to my right with an irrigation system at work. In front of me, where one of the pipes is leaking, a puddle has formed. A thirsty hare has stopped to take a drink. With my engine running I take just one shot, and move on to leave it in peace. I must admit it is the first and only time I have ever seen a hare drinking.

5th August

After two days of rain I should have known better; I got stuck on Barsham Breck Field yet again! Soil up to the axle, wheels spinning like my head, mud splattered up over the windows, and neither hare nor farmer in sight. I can't ask the farm manager or Richard the gamekeeper for help again as it has happened too many times – what a pain. After searching the hedgerows for over an hour, I find enough large flints and logs to put under the wheels so I can jack it up. Finally, after another hour of messing around I reverse out only to find a blown exhaust where a flint has pierced the pipe.

The sun is now up and starting to dry out the land; what a waste of half a day. I crash over stubble, back onto the track, with my windows down. All I need is a bit of drum and bass blasting out. I drive down the lane with its wide grass margins, tall, scraggy hedges and protruding Oaks. As I turn the corner, a young hare runs off in the distance, followed by a small group of Grey Partridges. As I get closer I can see that they were all dust bathing. What a shot that would have been. I drive back up the track for 100 yards, anchor the car sideways on, and wait. And it pays off. With the car still camouflaged in mud, the partridges come back two and a half hours later, followed by the hare, and settle down to dust bathe. I wait a while before I take my shots, and then I just sit and observe for the rest of the afternoon until they move off.

6th August

Got my flask of Earl Grey mixed with slices of ginger, a habit from being out in Africa. I have driven around a few estates and nothing. Down some of the old cart tracks, still nothing. I swing the car through a gateway and try to balance the wheels so as not to disappear down one of the dried up tractor furrows. The car slips and down it crashes. I come to a halt. I manage to reverse it out with a terrible tearing sound and I am back on top of the track. I get out, only to find all of the plastic underneath the car pulled away. It takes some time to rip it off and throw it into the boot to join all the other small pieces that have been knocked off over time. I suddenly notice that I am being watched by a young Roe buck, who suddenly takes flight. The day did not get much better.

12th August

I am now on a ferry with my daughter heading out to Oransay in the Hebrides to stay with some very good friends, Mike and Val, and drink Nelson's Blood! It's time to turn my back on the world, let go of the wheel and chill out. But it did not stop me yesterday from driving around my patch with my camera to check up on the hares. The past seven months have been a little hectic. I have now run into a brick wall with all the demands and requests and filming wish lists that needed satisfying yesterday!

When I get back I just want some time to watch the harvest. I called Richard from Oban and they still have to cut several fields due to the recent rain. I appreciate how lucky I was to have those six weeks in February and March to study the hares from dawn to dusk. The seasons are running away, the Blackberries are turning, Sloes forming, and the Grey Squirrels are on the Cobs and Beech mast. Soon I will be driving once again down the tram lines over the stubble fields. The Pink-footed Geese will be landing in from Iceland. Ah, to slow life's clock down.

30th August

I have wanted to do this all year. For once I am at home for harvest, not away filming on location, which is so often the case. I phone the farm manager and the head keeper to discuss what I would like to do and, with their blessing, I head out down the farm tracks. In the distance I can see the dust being kicked out by the combine harvester over the top of the hawthorn hedges. As I ease up through the gate posts and pull up by one of the tractors with the trailer for wheat, I am met by one of the farm hands. We chat for a while and out of the corner of my eye I can see the odd hare darting here and there. I want to get going.

As I drive around the outside of the field which had just been cut, it takes me a while to get into the zone, into the mindset of the hare, which has lived peacefully in these fields for the past eight months. Now this machine is cutting down their rain forest; think 'Avatar'. It has been their protection from man, predators from above and has sheltered them from wind, rain and sun. It has been their sanctuary and within a few hours it will be gone, a completely new landscape. This has been going on for thousands of years, with hand scythe, horse-drawn cutting equipment and now modern day machinery. It just gets bigger and cuts the corn faster.

Dust is everywhere and it's hard not to get it in the car and onto the camera equipment. I try to get the car into the right position each time, giving the combine enough room to turn at the end of each cut and not to be in the way of the two tractors with trailers or the tractor with the bailer.

I have filmed this before but never had the chance to pick up my stills camera. Here I am in my element, looking down a furrow with a combine bearing down on me; dust everywhere and the drone of the machinery. Suddenly a hare appears down the line, running towards me. I am invisible as it sprints past. I move to my next position and four hares break cover. Some sit to take in what is happening, some run for the hedge, while others wait until the very last moment. More often than not the hares run back to the ever-decreasing cornfield only to have to run out across the blades once more. I spend my whole day with the farmers, cutting several fields and taking several hundred photographs. I am looking forward to a soak in hot bath. I will see if Rachel and Sarah would like to join me in the fields tomorrow.

31st August

My friends join me with food and drink in the car for the day. I know the routine, where to leave the car and how much distance to give the combine. We have hares running down the tram lines towards us and many times a hare will sit down right in front of us, the moment seeming to last a lifetime. Late in the afternoon we track across the fields. Rachel is happy with the images she is taking, new ideas for her paintings and book. Sarah is beside me keeping an eye out. In the new stubble she spots a leveret with a tractor and bailer bearing down on it. The leveret has literally had a very close shave and it does not run as Sarah picks it up. Later, once the bailer had done its job, we placed it back where we found it.

We drive along a tramline on the next field with a hare running beside us. I accelerate up to 35mph down the field and the hare pulls away doing at least 45! That's its top speed and I am running out of tramlines. The hare could easily jink to left or right but it wants to race. I have done this several times before, when it pits itself against me in the car. Running in parallel lines the hare always wins! What a day.

The following day I am out on my own for the last two fields to be cut that season. I have spent three days with the harvesting and see the last strip cut at the end of the day. It's time to say a big 'thank you' to everyone. I have learnt a lot and if I were to film again, I would do it completely differently. But that's it for another year.

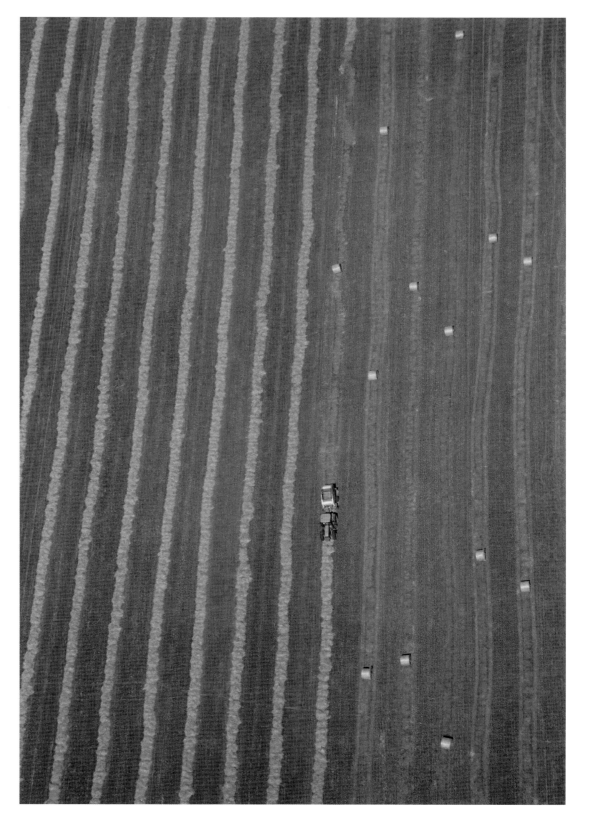

Autumn

12th September

Today I have Megan with me, observing hares together. I've come to know and love some hares, especially 'No Lugs', whose ear-tips were sliced off by a combine harvester many moons ago. From an early age leverets are able to play dead, freezing in one spot instead of fleeing when faced with danger. He now comes up to me quite closely and settles down to wash and clean. He's a great character and I really hope he makes it though to the next season.

18th September

I can't help but smile when I see the first geese fly in from across the North Sea, the end of a long journey from their northern breeding grounds; arriving skein after skein, in family groups, calling out as they go. For me this is the sign of autumn. These geese will build up in numbers to some 100,000 to over-winter in North Norfolk. Their first landing strips are normally the vast acres of stubble fields to eat the knocked down grains. It will be several weeks before the sugar beet are lifted, their favourite food.

20th September

Had a blast at a ska gig last night and met someone; someone special I think. You never know who may cross your path, maybe a new chapter in my life. I have been writing for days now and am starting to get cabin fever, so this afternoon I had a quick drive out in the evening sunlight. I only managed to see one hare out on the flint-strewn fields. I wonder if they ever tear open the pads on the bottom of their feet when they are running at speed across the sharpened stones. I know I get enough punctures.

27th September

Megan came out with me today and she was the first one to spot the returning skein of Pink-footed Geese high in a blue sky. In the warmth of the Indian summer, we both watched a Brimstone butterfly flutter by.

At the far end of North Pool, we pulled up, switched off the engine and waited. John had left a strip of barley for Simon's partridges to use for cover and food; it was not long before we were rewarded with a young hare coming out of one of the tram lines. It stretched its long frame, keeping his wary eye on us the whole time.

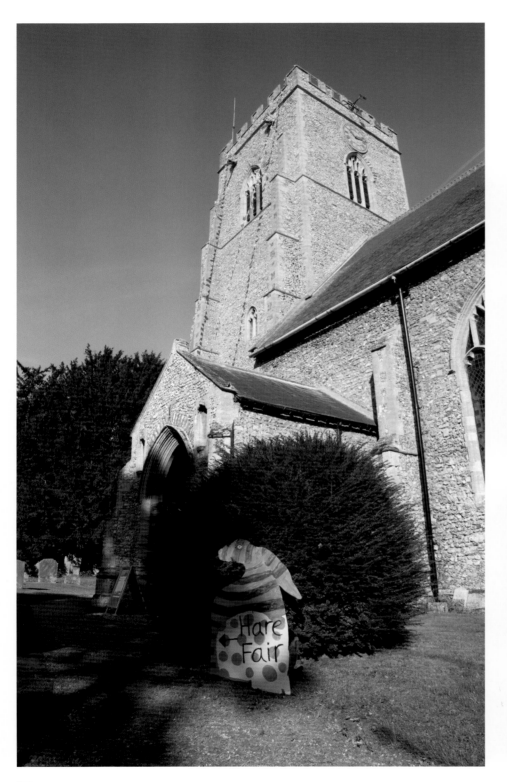

29th September

Saw an article in the Eastern Daily Press advertising a Hare Fair at Docking, in aid of the church. The land around Docking is well known for its hares, and also the Hare family, which has been associated with the village over many generations. The Fair is supported by local craft people, artist Nicole Hart, Holkham Forge, and many more. It is a great chance for those who like gifts that are a bit unusual and I came away with a few unique pieces.

5th October

Another grey day, with fog hanging in the air, giving an autumnal chill. I just needed to get out and go for a stomp, time to think and have space. I had not gone far when I could hear geese above, circling around calling, lost in the fog. As I walked, my boots laden with mud, it was not long before the silence was again broken, this time by the sound of twelve-bores from another pheasant shoot. The beaters worked in my favour, as from out of the mist hares appeared, sprinting towards me only to bolt the other way when they were almost on top of me. By then so were the beaters, so time to disappear into the fog.

6th October

A two-and-a-half-week-old leveret was passed to me by my friend, David. He already has a menagerie of injured birds and mammals about his house, so now it's my turn to experience a hare about the house.

The leveret is the only survivor of three youngsters attacked by a dog in their nest. The other two where killed instantly. This young lady has made it, but only just. David took her to the vet, where an X-ray showed that her back leg was broken below the knee. She wouldn't accept a splint, which was actually making the situation worse, causing her to thrash around and hold the leg at an even more unnatural angle. Nature will have to take its course.

When they called by and asked if I wanted to look after the hare at weekends, I just had to accept. It's not every day this happens; the last one was a decade ago.

I have called her Harlene, meaning 'from the hare meadow'. For the time being she is content in her towel nest on the kitchen table while I do my writing. So long as the nest has a high ridge that she can put her back up against, like in a form, she feels quite secure and happy to sleep, wash and clean herself while being looked at by 'Harvey' the stuffed hare. I use him in the field to film covertly from a 'GoPro' camera in his chest. The only time Harlene becomes tame is when she clamps her mouth round the bottle teat to drink.

20th October

Had Harlene this weekend, and my, what a difference ten days make. The first thing I noticed was how mobile her back leg was, which seems to be healing well. She explored every nook and cranny downstairs, and had her nose into everything, inquisitively sniffing and taking in new smells. The black tips on her ears are becoming more prominent, and her features looking sharper.

In the evening I picked fresh, tender, short grass for her and both Megan and I where amazed at the loud grinding noise she made while eating. After either a bottle feed or chewing on grass, she would retire to the back of the sofa, where she would clean herself and rest up, safe in her space.

For the time being, she has free range of the house at night, as I cannot bear the thought of her being boxed-up. Mornings she would hear me moving around, and wait eagerly at the foot of the stairs for her seven o'clock feed. Soon she will be up the stairs, and then things will have to change. As I head down the hall, she is close by my heels, but stops where the kitchen starts, for Harlene does not like the wooden floor, which makes her legs slip out in all directions. So this acts as a barrier while I prepare her milk. She is now on three feeds a day. In the lounge all the grass has gone, and in its place are lots of droppings.

23rd October

Most years I am lucky enough to go on the family shoot with my camera. I want to get the perfect photograph of a covey of Grey Partridges starbursting over a gnarled, berry-laden hawthorn hedge. With the odd oak tree in the background, and stubble in the foreground. Oh, and a blue sky with a few wisps of white cloud and the sun on my back. Not too much to ask, but as each year passes I am either sitting in the wrong place or it's misty or pouring with rain. It always amuses me how hares will break cover through the hedge, running towards and past the guns and dogs as though invisible, while everybody looks skywards in anticipation of the pheasants.

27th October

Harlene is now bounding around the house, getting bigger and stronger, but she could still do with putting on a bit more weight. The ends of her ears are becoming more pointed, losing their roundness. Her eyes have started to get lighter in colour, but still a long way to go for that golden-brown sparkle of an adult. Harlene has reduced to two feeds a day, and hopefully in another couple of weeks or so she will be weaned off milk altogether, as this little bundle of joy is living with me full time now.

Fiona came around and sat on the floor, to be greeted by Harlene sniffing her, to see what new scents were on her clothing. The leveret clambered over Fiona's lap, and then around behind her to start chewing on her belt, leaving some nice tooth marks in the leather.

At feeding time, it's still amazing to see how much suction there is on the bottle, and I can quite understand why I see adult mothers in the field boxing young leverets off. There comes a time when enough is enough. Sometimes I wonder while feeding her if it is true that they only feed once a day in the wild. Is there another feed before sun-up? This little one can really put it away.

After feeding, Harlene will sometimes find a sunny position in the lounge and sleep. With her legs tucked underneath and with no form to rest against, it looks as if she is going to roll to one side. It's like watching someone falling asleep on a train; head slowly sinking downwards only to suddenly jerk back. I must admit that I have never observed a wild hare sleeping. I have sat for hours watching them in their forms at a distance, but they always had one eye on me.

On one occasion the leveret made it across the wooden floor. To her this must have seemed like crossing an ice rink. The kitchen door was open to the elements and she sat there for a while, sniffing the cool breeze and gazing out onto the garden. I could see what was going to happen next, and it did. She hopped outside, so I put her into the temporary enclosure for the rest of the day, away from any cats. And from now on, doors closed.

31st October

It is still frosty as I drive onto a field that I have driven across many times. I pass through the gates and just sit there, surveying the landscape with binoculars. There is no need to go further as I have a perfect view before me. I have often sat here in the hope of seeing the elusive blue hare. I have never given up on it, for out there somewhere, hidden away from human eyes, it lies in a secret form. They say an adult hare's life span is normally three to four years. From my right Grey Partridges approach. I take a few shots and have one last glance over the field before I leave.

2nd November

It's quarter to six in the morning, blowing a hooley, and I've just dropped my daughter off at Morston sailing school for her instructors' course. On the way back in the dark I notice a bunch of hares silhouetted out on East Barsham Hill, so I rush home for camera and tripod and head back to the location. I switch off the engine and lights as I glide down the hill and ram the car up the verge. Lucky for me the wind is in the right direction as I stalk up the hill towards a handful of hares going about their business.

You have to remember that hares are nocturnal, feeding under the cover of darkness. I get as close as I dare to the brow of the hill before placing the tripod down, already at the right height with camera attached. I take a few photographs of them completely unaware of my presence and retreat down the hill, still in the dark. I cannot help hoping that Megan passes her test in these high gusting winds.

3rd November

A skittish hare powers itself forward just in front of me, using its hind legs to thrust its agile body onwards on large back feet.

5th November

Yesterday I spent most of the day writing but as the sun started to go down I had to escape. I drove my normal route but by the time I had stopped, started and peered through hedges, scouring the landscape for hares in forms or indeed any movement, the sun was disappearing fast. I drove back onto the road and then pulled into a gateway. Down a track beside the stubble field in front of me was a pair of Grey Partridges. As my fuel gauge flashed empty, I glided to a stop, the sun now down over the horizon. The stubble field on my right seemed as if it was moving and then I heard that beautiful sound of Grey Partridges calling. I lost count after 45 as they came so close. I was completely in my element, so much so that when I went to refuel I put petrol into my diesel car! Luckily I only put a quarter of a tank in, realized my mistake and finished filling up with diesel.

6th November

Here I am this morning in the early sunshine, with a car coughing and spluttering, looking for the large covey of partridges in the same place. I have a pair of Skylarks battling it out for song supremacy, red-legs calling out everywhere. The hedge is alive with Yellowhammers and I am pleased to see a flock of Tree Sparrows moving along with them. Time for me to move on, if the car starts!

10th November

Now seven weeks old, Harlene is on one bottle feed a day, and as well as eating grass in the outside pen, I have introduced lettuce and kale to her diet which has been enjoyed with much relish. Carrots with their green tops don't get touched, but the real treat is sweet parsnips, that get munched up by her growing teeth. When in the house, with her leg well on the mend, she can climb the stairs, giving her a new area to explore. I see her study her reflection in the mirror; one day she will do this on the edge of a drinking pool. Whether it's the carpet or sofa, Harlene will stop in any sunny spot in the cottage, snooze and soak up the warmth. Outside there are new sounds and sights to get used to, as she eats and washes herself.

14th November

After watching her leaping antics in the cottage, it was time to build a new enclosure; bigger, higher and with an overhang. She also has a new box with a slightly sloped roof, with dust-free hay inside for bedding. From the top windows I can still observe what she is up to. Harlene has now made a form under the metal seat, which she spends a lot of time in, surrounded by tall grass. When ever a Magpie flies over calling, she will sink down and lie flat, with ears held horizontal on her back. She has started to do this with humans, including me, which is pleasing to see.

15th November

Many days I will see a hare run across a field and trace it back to a hole at the base of a hedge, through which they disappear into the foliage and out onto the neighbouring field. This is where I will sit amongst the hawthorn and nettles some three metres away from the gap, in camouflaged clothes trying my best to blend in. Which side I sit on depends on the wind direction, so the hare doesn't pick up my scent.

16th November

Another day, the only decision being which way to head out. So I go up to the high hill, past a beautiful back-lit expanse of stubble sparkling in the morning sunlight, to find nothing but an empty field. I carry on up to the top of the lane, the odd Red-legged Partridge running in front of the vehicle. For some unknown reason I turn the car around, switch off the engine and free-wheel down the hill. This is fun, and as I cruise stealthily towards the back-lit stubble field, I squeeze the brakes down hard. There is my painting with light, a hare sitting up in the middle of the stubble, surrounded by shimmering cobwebs. You just know when you have taken a photograph of art. I drove home with Gogol Bordello blaring out from the speakers as the car pogos in and out of the potholes down the track. I was happy.

18th November

Having the hare about the house is beginning to take its toll. Believe me she's great fun, but by now you may be thinking where does it go to the loo? The droppings are everywhere, which is okay but they don't show you cleaning that in the Dyson adverts! There are urine puddles and stains on sofas, carpets, and all manner of unexpected places.

She is now leaping up the stairs at great speed, and if she hears me going up, then it's a game of getting to the top before me, getting under my feet to try and trip me up. This can be interesting with a tray of tea.

Harlene has taken to jumping on the windowsills to sniff the lilies and candelabra, both of which I'm surprised have not ended up on the floor. Thankfully the windows were only ajar, as it's rather a long way down! One habit has not stopped, and that is wherever I sit down, she will clamber over me and sniff my nose or mouth for a few seconds before settling.

The hare has even taken to sleeping under my bed. The dog has been kicked out, while Harlene has a lavish lifestyle, eating her kale and chilling out in front of the log burner. It's just like the Mad Hatter's Tea Party!

19th November

Came in late after a busy shoot, and was greeted by the hare sitting on the arm of the settee. After putting the kettle on, picking up the post, checking the answer phone, I sat in my office, to go though the e-mails. There have been many times in the last few weeks when I have thought this or that has been moved or nudged, but I glance down at Harlene and shake my head, for I know it can't be her. Maybe it was my daughter. Then suddenly that was all dismissed. There was a thundering down the hallway, and the next thing Harlene turned the corner at speed, leapt onto the bags and cases, and was there in front of me on my worktop. She clambered over paperwork, on top of photographs, knocked over cards on the window sill and generally pushed things around. The final straw was hopping onto the key pad, and sniffing the live wires; she has been up here before. Thank goodness she did not go to the loo, or chew the cables. Time for her to go back to her natural environment.

22nd November

I have been in rather a quandary as to where to release Harlene. It seems ridiculous that Megan and I watch hares just yards from the cottage, but know we can't release her here because there is hare shooting.

I was thinking of letting her go on Blakeney Point, as I remember seeing James McCallum's paintings of hares out there. If you go on-line there are photographs of them amongst the grasses. But after many discussions with Fiona it was decided not to. Then I remembered the gamekeeper who is guardian of the corvid roost at Bucken   ham. I have been there many times with many different presenters to film this spectacular event, and I had spoken to Jo about hares. He told me that he did not shoot them on his patch.

24th November

A bit of planning went into this shot, well before the frost. I often spotted the Barn Owl working the meadow and always landing on the same perch. So after finding a gnarled old post I decorated it with some rusty barbed wire. On hearing that there would be another hard frost the following day I went into the meadow and swapped the posts over. Low and behold, it all went like clockwork. I got my shots, replaced the original perch and put the barbed wire post up against my house, where it joined the twenty other posts that will come in handy one day.

26th November

Rachel came over today and it was great to share an amazing experience with a fellow artist. I paint using light with my cameras, but watching Rachel with her pencil flowing over a blank canvas, drawing hare studies from life really is a revelation.

28th November

It came as no surprise to see the Pink-footed Geese in front of Burnham Overy windmill. I am always driving around, making notes where the sugar beet fields are, so it is nice to get geese into a Norfolk landscape. The birds fly to and fro; to the marsh for a wash and scrub-up before flying back to the harvested fields to feed on the scraps that have been left. Whether it's leaves or beet, the farm machinery gets more efficient so there is less for the birds to eat.

30th November

Today is the release day for Harlene and don't I know it. It's a hell of a wrench but it's got to be done. I went for an early morning walk and it started to drizzle hard, but it didn't stop a female Sparrowhawk flying by on a mission into the nearby spinney. A cloud of pigeons rose into the sky, and no doubt amongst the trees there was a cloud of feathers floating on the wind. Once back at Ticketyboo Cottage, I went on-line and checked all the weather forecasts. It was just a squall blowing though, and the rest of the day should stay fine.

I got the last of the kale, broccoli and cut sprouts from the fridge, and took them out to the pen for her last high-protein feed. I also bagged up a road-kill hare, to drop of to the taxidermist near Norwich, to do a Harvey Mark 2.

Harlene hopped into her travelling box, and then Megan and I were on the road to Buckenham. It was good to see Jo again, and I reiterated concerns about hare shooting, to be assured that even the neighbouring farms do not kill hares.

We walked past the church, and out into the sugar beet field, which would be good cover from raptors and the weather. I handed Megs the camera, and placed the container down into the tram line. As soon as Harlene came out of the box, her senses kicked in and she was sniffing the leaves and the soil. Then she took a look around to observe the skyline. And with that, she sunk down into the vegetation, and was gone.

I wished her a good journey and a safe passage, and at that moment a rainbow appeared. I smiled inwardly. It had been a magical journey sharing a small part of her life.

Winter

6th December

I thought this was 'No Lugs' today. I really had to look hard, but after a while I convinced myself it was not. All the different characters I have got to know and observe on their turf will change in a few months time when the hare shoots start in February. It is reputed that in East Anglia alone over a quarter of a million hares are shot in one month. In one day's shooting most estates will kill between 250 and 500 hares, and last year it was rumoured that one estate shot 913 in a single day. However, I do know of a good number of estates that no longer shoot hares on their land, which must be good news.

10th December

I took Megan to UEA to go climbing. It was a crisp morning with a fresh breeze and I could not help scouring the land as were travelling. We clocked dead Badgers on the road sides, along with Roe Deer. We had our eye on a Red Deer yesterday but someone had beaten us to it when we went back for it. As the sun was coming up I had to stop and take this photograph of the Rooks playing in the wind. I do admire their canny aerobatic skills. We passed several rookeries with the Rooks taking up position on last year's nests.

11th December

Cutting across the Norfolk landscape early on this hoar-frosty morning in pursuit of hares, I came across a pack of hounds, the North Norfolk Harriers, being exercised. It's strange to think that dogs like these were used for hunting hares since way back in 1871, but at least no more. I carried on down the track with its vista of ice crystals and frozen dew drops in search of my quarry.

12th December

Listening to all the weather stations and watching forecast charts on-line, it seems we are due for heavy snow falls. Time to dig out thermals and snow boots, and make sure all camera batteries are charged up, before heading out later that day. It is a case of phoning Richard to find out if there are any shoots, which stubble field I would like to sit in and where I had last seen some hares.

With that sorted, and flask of tea in hand, I head out down the lanes and out onto the fields. There is no sun, just a slate grey sky and a brisk north–easterly, so I make sure that I'm not facing into the wind. I don't want hares in my sights and wet snow on the front of the lens. I move into position with window down, bean bag on the door and camera in place, all before I stop moving. Then switch off the engine, and sit motionless. Once again, like every day, the waiting begins.

In the far distance shotguns can be heard. High above me I can hear Pink-footed Geese calling out to each other, searching for a recently harvested sugar beet field and sanctuary.

At long last a light snow flurry and with the light falling fast, I move my gloved hand slowly up to the camera and compose my subjects in the frame. Not only a stationary hare but three more running in from the left, a pair of Grey Partridges on my right, and then it stops snowing. Everything clears off without a bye or leave. I look to my left and right, a blank canvas. Time for a cup of tea.

13th December

The first winter snow has drifted in and has hit hard with a biting cold northerly wind. I tried to get onto the fields, but it is so wet underneath the snow the wheels were spinning and I could feel the old girl sinking in. I will have to stick to the lanes for now but I can see the hares out in the fields, out of reach. A few words came to mind; I will have to put down 'damn and blast', but I can tell you it was a bit stronger than that! At the end of the day I came across a flock of Lapwings facing into the harsh winds as another snow-storm blasted in. They stood fast, anchored down with safety in numbers. I crept the car on past as I did not want to be stuck for the night.

14th December

Snowing hard though the night, as I head up Barsham Hill. I can see where other cars have slid to one side and I knew it would be fatal to stop, but I just had to photograph this Woodcock in the middle of the road. It's now a full moon and these birds will fly over on a moon-lit night from Scandinavia, supposedly for an easier winter! I take my shots and put the car into reverse, heading all the way back down to the bottom, only to charge at the hill again. Once down the lanes I try to go off piste down the cart tracks, but it's no good as the snow is too deep. It's so tantalising, as I can see hares out in the middle of the field in the drifting snow. I stare long and hard down the tunnel of gnarled old hawthorns and feel as if I'm

being drawn into its path. I can see where those have gone before me, like the Land of Narnia, but my wheels are spinning. For once common sense prevails as I head back up the lanes, but not before I stop to observe the Rooks searching for food. Life is going to get a lot tougher for us all with the harshness of winter blowing in.

15th December

The gang catching up with all the news at the end of the day!

16th December

The cold continues unabated. I picked up a dead Barn Owl today, its breast bone is as sharp as a blade, with no meat on it. All the voles are underneath the snow-covered landscape and this is the sixth owl I know about that has died in this parish alone. The population will take many years to recover from this winter.

17th December

I heard a tale today from a friend about a keeper we both know. He was driving around the headlands when a Sparrowhawk went screaming past along the hedge, and put up a covey of Grey Partridges. The hawk took one of them in mid-flight and the rest of the covey landed some 40 metres in the distance. After about 15 seconds the covey took off again and flew back to where the predator was sitting on its lunch. Taken by surprise, the hawk took off leaving its startled prey to get up and fly away with the covey.

Christmas Day

A day off; a day off to enjoy with my daughter and family. I got a beautiful sculpture of a life-size running hare from Fiona which I shall have to find a special place for. At Meg's request we went for an afternoon walk down at Brancaster Beach. It was blowing a hooley with the sand being swept along and my daughter lying down amongst it trying to capture its movement. On the drive back we saw skeins of Pink-footed Geese in the wintery salmon sky. I could not help but drive down one of the cart tracks to do a bit of hare spotting before Christmas lunch.

30th December

Today brought a lull in the bad weather and a respite for the hares. I had my earliest sighting of hares mating to date, so she will be giving birth in the first week of February. I sat with these hares for sometime and the buck that was mating with the doe could not let his guard down. He kept an eye on the male to his left, who kept on coming in to challenge. This was to no avail, as the dominant male would box the weaker one and chase him off. But it did not stop him trying again and again, until she called an end to it by taking flight.

New Year's Day

A fuzzy head, and that's putting it lightly; why did I hit those sloe gins? But had a great time with friends at the Morston Anchor. Fiona decided to take her dog for a walk across the field to blow away a few cobwebs. At least the dog seemed keen. I waved goodbye to my glowing wood burner and Laurence of Arabia on the box (one day I will get to watch the whole film). With camera in hand, off we went. It was not long before the terrier put up a hare amongst the stubble. We then stood still with dog by our feet as a hare ran straight towards us. Maybe this is what they call the hare of the dog! Well, it worked for me.

4th January

Went back to try to find the hares from yesterday. The ground was still frozen, letting me drive back over the stubble field, seeing nothing except the coolant light flashing at me. On to the next field and the odd hare snuggled down in their forms. I took one or two photos but then let them be as they were having a hard enough time as it was. I then glanced upwards and there, with out-stretched bodies and slow wing beats, were seven cranes heading west. So random, just like the lights flashing on my dashboard.

5th January

Heard a rumour that someone thought they had seen a different coloured hare, on the north high hills. Could this really be the blue hare that I have searched in vain for and not seen for nearly a year? It really is like searching for the Holy Grail.

I push my poor old car even harder over the rough, frozen terrain in anticipation from this new lead. Again I scan the land with my eyes pressed hard into my binoculars, but to no avail. The north wind has a freezing edge to it and nothing moves. For once the blue hare would, if still alive, dissolve into its surroundings, amongst the ruts of snow. I observe every hare that put its head above the parapet, only to shake my head again.

6th January

Another relentless blast of Arctic snow. I dare not go down any farm tracks; it's bad enough just driving on B-roads that have not been gritted in North Norfolk. As I head up to Brancaster across the high ridge, I listen to the radio. Major roads have ground to a halt, airports closed, hundreds of schools have shut down, farmers have had to dig sheep out from snow drifts and some people have died from hypothermia. Conditions really are treacherous, yet I feel compelled to be out amongst it all capturing the moment. I stop to take photographs of snow-covered sheep, but I have to press on. It's not long before I reach my destination; the cultivated acres of sugar beet. I find an entrance in the hedge with a slope leading back onto the road, ideal if I get stuck as I can roll back. To my right a pheasant in the field margin does not seem too disturbed by my presence. Set out in front of me, several thousand Pink-footed Geese are trying to find food in the snow.

7th January

A filming assignment for the BBC's 'Snow Watch' takes us over to Strumpshaw Fen, with Megan acting as my camera assistant. Megs counted 61 hares out on this field, which where all content until a Chinese Water Deer ran in from the left. I must admit I have never seen so many hares together in one place.

8th January

Grey Partridges have to dig deep under the frozen snow for food just to survive.

9th January

The big freeze. It's now quite easy to see where the hares have been, their footprints navigating paths across the vast white landscape. Quite soon I find some in their frozen forms. I do admire these amazing creatures, for they can take all that the weather throws at them. Their only shelter a scrape in the open fields, braving Arctic conditions which at night fall below –9 degrees.

10th January

Clear blue skies today, after a star-lit night, so the ground is frozen first thing. I knew where I want to be, so at first light I went for it. Unfortunately the snow was not as solid as I thought it was going to be. Life ground to a halt on the first sunny day for ages. I could see hares in the distance while I tried to dig out my car with a plate, but it was no use. It was going to have to be an embarrassing call to Richard to tow me out. It was from there that I drove to the Brecks, to have a drive round with Chris in his 4x4. It was not long before we found hares, and also male Grey Partridges fighting over females. At least the day was not wasted.

A Breckland hare.

11th January

With the raw cold comes different behaviour patterns. As I drive down the old cart tracks, I stop to take photographs of Woodcock feeding only metres away from me. I also pass young hares just sitting motionless, trying to blend in amongst the hedgerows, conserving energy for the night's foraging ahead. A friend, David Lewis, tells me of coming across a dozen or so hares at night on top of a mound of sugar beet, where they were munching away on the roots just to survive.

12th January

Today started badly. Feeling decidedly groggy at six in the morning; my tea drunk, toast eaten, warm clothes fitted but no car. I forgot that last night a friend gave me a lift home from the pub. What's more, when I looked out of the window I found a fresh fall of heavy snow. After the two mile walk to the pub I came back home, picked up my camera gear and set off.

By now the sun had risen and was reflecting off the snow, blinding my fragile eyes and making me wish I'd stuck to shandy. As I arrived at Martha's Field I saw two large hares run towards the copse. Just as I was about to drive to another spot I noticed what looked like a clod of earth sticking out of the snow, like a mole hill. After many years you know better, so I drove my poor old jalopy across the field. As I got ever closer, it hunkered down, relying on the misguided idea that I couldn't see it. I pulled up to the pretend clod and I could see yet another mound in the distance. All that moved was a charm of Goldfinches working the dead seed heads along the field margins.

13th January

Heading up to the coast, sticking to the gritted tarmac, it's not long before I'm sitting with a dozen hares in one field. They have already started to have disputes, chasing one another and getting frisky. My earliest date of watching them mate was on the 30th December, but they mate a lot earlier than that. The gestation period for a pregnant hare is normally 42 days, so come the shoots in February and March, there are many young orphaned leverets which are left to die of starvation.

14th January

After a wild night I opened the window to let the early morning light in. Frost lays across the meadow, and a Kingfisher's cry pierces the silence. It's time to kick people out and crack on with the day. As I drive down a long single track with grassy verges and tall hawthorn hedges each side, there in front of me is a male Sparrowhawk. I am right on his tail, at 35 mph, for over a quarter mile. Using the car as cover, a Blackbird lifts up from the grass on my left and flies into the hedge and the hawk glides in after it. The Mozart on the radio is very fitting to the scene; *Exsultate, Jubilate*.

15th January

Fieldfares and Redwings feast upon the abundant crop of red, rich Hawthorn berries down the narrow winding tracks. This in turn makes ideal feeding grounds for the hunter, the stealth, the Sparrowhawk.

16th January

As there are pheasant shoots across the land I cannot frequent my usual haunts. I woke early this morning and headed straight for Holkham in the still freezing temperatures. I intended to get some more wintery shots of Pink-footed Geese, but instead I chanced upon these hares and a group of Brent Geese huddled together for warmth and safety in numbers.

17th January

With thermal layers, snow boots, Russian hat and a rucksack, I head out into the chilled air down the lanes, with Fieldfares flying high above. It's not long before I'm sitting in a hedge on one of the rises, gazing out onto the vista, just sitting and taking in the big picture, with hares running free in the foreground. These majestic creatures have been here for about 2,000 years, some say introduced by the Romans, originating from the grasslands of central Asia. I hope they are here for many years to come, to give future generations the chance to gaze upon the elegance of these sleek, spiritual creatures.

18th January

Finally the thaw arrives, and the countryside is starting to revert back to normal after such adverse conditions. I can hear a woodpecker drumming, and seeing the Barn Owl hunting down one of the tracks puts a smile on my face. I must order a couple more nest boxes for them from the Sculthorpe Moor Nature Reserve, as they are going to need all the help they can get.

19th January

The snow starts to recede, hare tracks across the stubble fields now become more visible. Some hares can be seen standing up on their hind legs surveying the land. You can see why these creatures were once steeped in mystery, folklore and magic. They were reputed to be associated with witches, for their ability to either appear or disappear in the blink of an eye.

20th January

It's now my last chance to go out onto the stubble fields before they get ploughed in, and a new crop sown. It's the circle of life, ever changing, and nothing stops or stays the same. I pull up to a hare in a form with my 300mm lens at the ready. Its nose twitched, its long whiskers stayed still, its eye is a picture within itself. As ever, I take only a few shots and move on, for his form is soon to be no more.

21st January

Just great to have three hares so close to observe. They were at one with each other, as there was no sniffing of each other or boxing. It was hard to tell who was female or male. There was nothing to feed on, as it was a ploughed field, but now and again one would wash itself, while the others watched on. It was like they had a mutual understanding, and it was one of those times you would like to know what on earth was going on.

All was okay until they stared to their right. I looked to my left and another hare was running in. It stopped about a metre away from the three, and began to stretch in a beautiful arc. Was this all a ploy, as it then stretched forward to sniff the scent of the group? With that the other three were off over the rise of the hill, the fourth hare in hot pursuit. The Skylark carried on singing high above.

24th January

A hard frost, and I've been told of hares eating knocked-down sweet corn cobs. So a very early start to put up my hide in the dark. At day break I just have pigeons and Rooks feeding in front of me, with the odd Pheasant passing by. In my three foot cubicle it gives me time to reflect, and I wonder how Harlene is getting on in her new home. I am so pleased that she was released in a sugar beet field, as it has not been lifted yet due to the weather. So there is plenty of food and cover. I come away from the hide after dusk with not a hare in sight. Well, there's always tomorrow.

26th January

I had to smile to myself today. Whilst out hunting for hares, I came across a tractor bogged down in the mud. It makes a change to see someone else stuck and not me!

27th January

Watched this pair of hares boxing and scrapping and it was not until they finished that I noticed what the female had done to the male with her claws. The topside of his flank was slashed and bleeding, which is not uncommon. I have been told of male hares that have been found dead, having bled to death after fights where they have been castrated by the female.

30th January
Pink-footed Geese in the setting sun.

31st January
Wild Pink-footed Goose chase.

3rd February

Spot the hare.

5th February

One of my great joys is to find a fresh, empty form and to sit and wait, sometimes for hours, until the owner returns.

6th February

A low winter sun, and a harsh wind that cuts across the open fields. However this hare has found a refuge next to the solid trunk on the leeward side, as it soaks up the warmth of the morning glow.

7th February

In my hide early this morning with flask of tea, and double skinned with warm clothes and boots. It's still not sun up, and a frost covers the lower land. I am cramped and tight within my cubicle, but it is a happy place to be today, far from the madding crowd. After several hours, as the sun burnt though the clouds, I was rewarded with many shots, some of the golden hare.

8th February

Soon the Hawthorn hedges will be bursting out into lush green, a real sense of the earth awakening. Sometimes you know that you have to put the hours in watching nature and sometimes it is more luck than judgment. This evening was amazing. I could see the Barn Owl in the distance, heading towards me. I swung the car across the path as it carried on gliding towards me, with Grey Partridges on the brow of the hill and pheasants to my left. Usually it doesn't get much better than this, but today it did. Three hares burst through the hedge on my right, stayed for all of 30 seconds and then give chase through the hedge to the left. I put the camera down as the owl floated by and the partridges called out in the evening light. What a magical experience to have so much going on in one frame.

9th February

John decided to leave this field fallow, which made for great wildlife cover and great photo opportunities! It was by pure chance that I found this leveret. I was by the side of the field to stretch my legs after being in the car all day, when four Bullfinches flicked out of the hedge, white rumps flashing as they went. I looked down and noticed a little dumpling at my feet. There was no sign of mum, who would not be back until evening time to feed. Alone, leverets rely completely on their camouflage for protection. Sadly this strategy doesn't always work. Farm machinery roars on regardless, while predators including raptors, crows, opportunistic Foxes and Stoats plus dogs and cats all take their toll. Curiosity got the better of me and I needed to know just how close I could get. The answer is that I could have counted the hairs on its nose.

27th February

Another season draws to an end as the Pink-footed Geese take to the air in the changing wind on the long journey to their Icelandic breeding grounds. I am left pondering whether I carry on my search with the hares or will I tack and change course in life. I wonder what new challenges and quests lie ahead.

28th February
Spring has sprung.

29th February

Blue, Spring-like skies as I drive down familiar tracks on a hare safari. After many miles of slow driving down the country lanes it becomes only too clear that numbers are well down. In past years I have driven with them on the track ahead, or when I pulled the car into a field entrance, I would of seen half a dozen or more. I only have to put out a tweet, and the response is the same elsewhere. It saddens me to see the barren fields, where only a few seasons ago hares ran wild. After having put up with a very wet year, and bitterly cold winter, they have to survive the hare shoots when thousands of hares are slaughtered every February and early March when females are pregnant, or have just given birth. This leaves orphaned leverets to starve to death around the field margins. It is my belief, and for many others, that there should be a close season for the iconic hare, as in other mainland European countries when they can't be hunted, as it is for fishing, deerstalking, wild fowling, pheasants, partridges and grouse. If there was shooting at all, November would be the best season, when the females are less likely to be pregnant or have suckling young leverets in the field.

There are some responsible landowners who care about conservation and are happy to see hares on their land but, at the end of the day, we all need to be guardians of our wildlife and surrounding countryside to ensure that it will not be 'Hare today, gone tomorrow'.

27th March

Clocks have moved forward! Once again I am up and out, searching my patch on this dull, grey morning. I have driven around the estate and nudged onto the neighbouring one but all is quiet, so back to Barsham to hunt for a pair of hares.

My mobile rings. Richard has just been told by the under-keeper that he has seen the blue hare on Ed's Hill. I thought it was dead, but he told me not so. All down to good game-keeping. I had to smile and immediately I turned the car around and headed up to the 20-acre field, where the oilseed rape is now eight inches high. I must have driven around the field six times or more, as it had moved since the under-keeper last saw it. I texted Richard, who was searching in the knocked-down maize. He replied saying that it looked like it had been and gone. I was thinking that it cannot possibly be there after all this time. After another search though the binoculars I drive a further 10 metres up the field, and there, about 150 metres in, is a blob down one of the lines of rape. I size up the field. It is a Sunday and there is only one thing for it. A tram line runs close to the hare and if I can drive down the left hand side I could get close enough for some great footage. I need to find how the tractor got onto the field; no doubt the other side of the hill. Now driving down the tramline, with the rape almost a foot tall in places, I check around me to make sure that I am not doing any damage. By now I have driven all around the field and head up the chosen line. Guess what? Not a sign! The rape is too tall so I continue all the way down to the end, swing left onto the tractor marks and there it is, lying flat. I go down the line that is right next to it, hoping it won't run. I continue forward, camera rolling, pull up opposite, now only six metres away. I focus and hit 'record'. I am conscious that I am filming my first ever blue hare in East Anglia. I am able to get close ups, mids and wide angles. Happy with what I have managed to capture, I take some stills then back onto film. At which point up he gets up and hops out of the frame, heads to the hedge and disappears. I remained in place all day but he had gone. Finally giving up at dusk, I headed home to download my day's work. Wow, was I happy. I checked my notes. I had last seen him on 22nd March – a year and five days ago. I cannot believe he had only moved five fields but had remained elusive to three keepers, the farmer and all the tractor drivers.

I was elated with finding the Barsham blue hare after a year of scanning the land. To be able to just sit and look deep into those wise, golden eyes, if only for a short time, has been an amazing experience.

Just tickety-boo.

Martin Hayward Smith

When out in the field I always carry my diary in my rucksack, so I can make quick notes. When I'm writing I have to be in 'the zone'. I have several nearby locations I can drive to that help achieve this; the open vistas of the rolling Norfolk countryside are a great aid. At other times I just sit in my office to write, looking out of the window onto the lawn that goes down to the river Stiffkey. I will take a break and go stand on the jetty, throwing bread to feed the Brown Trout and to check if any Otters have sprainted. Sometimes while writing, I hear the call of the Kingfisher or the Barn Owl will fly past to feed its young in the nest box, dodging the Kestrel also feeding its young. Spotted Flycatchers sit in the old pear tree with butterflies in their beaks feeding their young. Grey Partridges visit the patio and Snipe fly in and out of the ditch. To date, I've had 61 species of bird land in my garden.

I was born and bred in North Norfolk. My father was a press photographer and keen sailor. From an early age I learned to sail at Brancaster, where exploring the creeks and sandbars and the nature that lived there probably started my love of wildlife.

At eight years old, my father began teaching me how to develop and print film in his dark room. I left home to join the Navy, and after five years travelling the world with camera in hand, I returned and started working for the oil industry in the North Sea, the Ivory Coast and Gabon. I've visited Africa many times and was lucky enough to meet and work with the late George Adamson of *Born Free* fame. A commission from Anglia Television followed and I joined the renowned *Survival* team as a wildlife cameraman, travelling the world from the crocodile caves of Madagascar to the Amazon basin.

This led to further filming commissions in many countries, from Madagascar, the Arctic Circle, Oman, Australia, USA, the Amazon Basin, Canada, Ghana, Kenya, Uganda, Tanzania and Peru but to name a few, and I continue to film for the BBC, ITV, Channel 5, Discovery, Japan, Channel 4, National Geographic, Disney and more.

When not filming, or hanging out of helicopters taking landscape photographs, I can be found on my houseboat amongst the salt marshes and creeks with my daughter and family, or sailing at Morston on the North Norfolk coast.

Ticketyboo Cottage

The holiday cottage, Old Beans Cottage, North Norfolk.
www.oldbeanscottage.co.uk

For more information about my work or if you'd like to get in touch: martinhaywardsmith@btinternet.com
www.martinhaywardsmith.com

Thank you to

Susanna and Jeremy Soames, Chris Knights, Richard Futter, Walsingham Estate, Simon Owen, David Carr, Lyn Leverett, Peter Smithson, Ian Forman, Gary Smith, Robbie and Sheree Cupper, Sarah Whittley and Ray Mears.